Apostolic Letter of
John Paul II
to the Bishops of
the Catholic Church

ON RESERVING PRIESTLY ORDINATION TO MEN ALONE

Ordinatio Sacerdotalis

BOOKS & MEDIA
Boston

No part of this booklet may be photocopied without written permission from the publisher.

English Translation: L'Osservatore Romano

ISBN 0-8198-5433-6

Copyright © 1994, Daughters of St. Paul

Printed and published in the U.S.A. by Pauline Books & Media, 50 Saint Pauls Avenue, Boston MA 02130-3491.

www.pauline.org

Pauline Books & Media is the publishing house of the Daughters of St. Paul, an international congregation of women religious serving the Church with the communications media.

3 4 5 6 7 8   06 05 04 03 02 01

Venerable Brothers in the Episcopate,

1. Priestly ordination, which hands on the office entrusted by Christ to his Apostles of teaching, sanctifying and governing the faithful, has in the Catholic Church from the beginning always been reserved to men alone. This tradition has also been faithfully maintained by the Oriental Churches.

When the question of the ordination of women arose in the Anglican Communion, Pope Paul VI, out of fidelity to his office of safeguarding the Apostolic Tradition, and also with a view to removing a new obstacle placed in the way of Christian unity, reminded Anglicans of the position of the Catholic Church: "She holds that it is not admissible to ordain women to the priesthood, for very fundamental reasons. These reasons include: the example recorded in the Sacred Scriptures of Christ choosing his Apostles only from among men; the constant practice of the Church, which has imitated Christ in choosing only men; and her living teaching authority which has consistently held that the exclusion of women from the priesthood is in accordance with God's plan for his Church."[1]

---

1. Paul VI, Response to the Letter of His Grace the Most Reverend Dr. F. D. Coggan, Archbishop of Canterbury, concerning the Ordination of Women to the Priesthood (November 30, 1975); *AAS* 68 (1976), 599.

But since the question had also become the subject of debate among theologians and in certain Catholic circles, Paul VI directed the Congregation for the Doctrine of the Faith to set forth and expound the teaching of the Church on this matter. This was done through the Declaration *Inter Insigniores*, which the Supreme Pontiff approved and ordered to be published.[2]

2. The Declaration recalls and explains the fundamental reasons for this teaching, reasons expounded by Paul VI, and concludes that the Church "does not consider herself authorized to admit women to priestly ordination."[3] To these fundamental reasons the document adds other theological reasons which illustrate the appropriateness of the divine provision, and it also shows clearly that Christ's way of acting did not proceed from sociological or cultural motives peculiar to his time. As Paul VI later explained: "The real reason is that, in giving the Church her fundamental constitution, her theological anthropology—thereafter always followed by the Church's Tradition—Christ established things in this way."[4]

In the Apostolic Letter *Mulieris Dignitatem*, I myself wrote in this regard: "In calling only men as his Apostles, Christ acted in a completely free and soveriegn manner. In doing so, he exercised the same freedom with which, in all his behavior, he emphasized the dignity and the vocation of women, without conforming to the prevailing customs and to the traditions sanctioned by the legislation of the time."[5]

---

2. Cf. Congregation for the Doctrine of the Faith, Declaration *Inter Insigniores* on the question of the Admission of Women to the Ministerial Priesthood (October 15, 1976): *AAS* 69 (1977), 98-116.

3. Ibid., 100

4. Paul VI, *Address on the Role of Women in the Plan of Salvation* (January 30, 1977): *Insegnamenti*, XV (1977), 111. Cf. also John Paul II Apostolic Exhortation *Christifideles laici* (December 30, 1988), n. 51: *AAS* 81 (1989), 393-521; *Catechism of the Catholic Church*, n. 1577.

5. Apostolic Letter *Mulieris Dignitatem* (August 15, 1988), n. 26: *AAS* 80 (1988), 1715.

In fact the Gospels and the Acts of the Apostles attest that this call was made in accordance with God's eternal plan; Christ chose those whom he willed (cf. Mk 3:13-14; Jn 6:70), and he did so in union with the Father, "through the Holy Spirit" (Acts 1:2), after having spent the night in prayer (cf. Lk 6:12). Therefore, in granting admission to the ministerial priesthood,[6] the Church has always acknowledged as a perennial norm her Lord's way of acting in choosing the twelve men whom he made the foundation of his Church (cf. Rv 21:14). These men did not in fact receive only a function which could thereafter be exercised by any member of the Church; rather they were specifically and intimately associated in the mission of the Incarnate Word himself (cf. Mt 10:1, 7-8; 28:16-20; Mk 3:13-16; 16:14-15). The Apostles did the same when they chose fellow workers[7] who would succeed them in their ministry.[8] Also included in this choice were those who, throughout the time of the Church, would carry on the Apostles' mission of representing Christ the Lord and Redeemer.[9]

3. Furthermore, the fact that the Blessed Virgin Mary, Mother of God and Mother of the Church, received neither the mission proper to the Apostles nor the ministerial priesthood clearly shows that the non-admission of women to priestly ordination cannot mean that women are of lesser dignity, nor can it be construed as discrimination against them. Rather, it is to be seen as the faithful observance of a plan to be ascribed to the wisdom of the Lord of the universe.

---

6. Cf. Dogmatic Constitution *Lumen Gentium*, n. 28: Decree *Presbyterorum Ordinis*, n. 2b.

7. Cf. 1 Tm 3:1-13; 2 Tm 1:6; Ti 1:5-9.

8. Cf. *Catechism of the Catholic Church*, n. 1577.

9. Cf. Dogmatic Constitution on the Church *Lumen Gentium*, nn. 20, 21.

The presence and the role of women in the life and mission of the Church, although not linked to the ministerial priesthood, remain absolutely necessary and irreplaceable. As the Declaration *Inter Insigniores* points out, "the Church desires that Christian women should become fully aware of the greatness of their mission: today their role is of capital importance both for the renewal and humanization of society and for the rediscovery by believers of the true face of the Church."[10]

The New Testament and the whole history of the Church give ample evidence of the presence in the Church of women, true disciples, witnesses to Christ in the family and in society, as well as in total consecration to the service of God and of the Gospel. "By defending the dignity of women and their vocation, the Church has shown honor and gratitude for those women who—faithful to the Gospel—have shared in every age in the apostolic mission of the whole People of God. They are the holy martyrs, virgins and mothers of families, who bravely bore witness to their faith and passed on the Church's faith and tradition by bringing up their children in the spirit of the Gospel."[11]

Moreover, it is to the holiness of the faithful that the hierarchical structure of the Church is totally ordered. For this reason, the Declaration *Inter Insigniores* recalls: "the only better gift, which can and must be desired, is love (cf. 1 Cor 12 and 13). The greatest in the Kingdom of Heaven are not the ministers but the saints."[12]

---

10. Congregation for the Doctrine of the Faith, Declaration *Inter Insigniores*, n. 6: *AAS* 69 (1977), 115-116.

11. Apostolic Letter *Mulieris Dignitatem*, n. 27:*AAS* 80 (1988), 1719.

12. Congregation for the Doctrine of the Faith, Declaration *Inter Insigniores*, n. 6:*AAS* 69 (1977), 115.

4. Although the teaching that priestly ordination is to be reserved to men alone has been preserved by the constant and universal Tradition of the Church and firmly taught by the Magisterium in its more recent documents, at the present time in some places it is nonetheless considered still open to debate, or the Church's judgment that women are not to be admitted to ordination is considered to have a merely disciplinary force.

Wherefore, in order that all doubt may be removed regarding a matter of great importance, a matter which pertains to the Church's divine constitution itself, in virtue of my ministry of confirming the brethren (cf. Lk 22:32) I declare that the Church has no authority whatsoever to confer priestly ordination on women and that this judgment is to be definitively held by all the Church's faithful.

Invoking an abundance of divine assistance upon you, venerable brothers, and upon all the faithful, I impart my apostolic blessing.

From the Vatican, on May 22, the Solemnity of Pentecost, in the year 1994, the sixteenth of my pontificate.

Joannes Paulus PP. II

BOOKS & MEDIA

The Daughters of St. Paul operate book and media centers at the following addresses. Visit, call or write the one nearest you today, or find us on the World Wide Web, www.pauline.org

California
3908 Sepulveda Blvd, Culver City, CA 90230   310-397-8676
5945 Balboa Avenue, San Diego, CA 92111   858-565-9181
46 Geary Street, San Francisco, CA 94108   415-781-5180

Florida
145 S.W. 107th Avenue, Miami, FL 33174   305-559-6715

Hawaii
1143 Bishop Street, Honolulu, HI 96813   808-521-2731

Neighbor Islands call: 800-259-8463

Illinois
172 North Michigan Avenue, Chicago, IL 60601   312-346-4228

Louisiana
4403 Veterans Memorial Blvd, Metairie, LA 70006   504-887-7631

Massachusetts
Rte. 1, 885 Providence Hwy, Dedham, MA 02026
781-326-5385

Missouri
9804 Watson Road, St. Louis, MO 63126   314-965-3512

New Jersey
561 U.S. Route 1, Wick Plaza, Edison, NJ 08817
732-572-1200

New York
150 East 52nd Street, New York, NY 10022
212-754-1110
78 Fort Place, Staten Island, NY 10301   718-447-5071

Ohio
2105 Ontario Street, Cleveland, OH 44115   216-621-9427

Pennsylvania
9171-A Roosevelt Blvd, Philadelphia, PA 19114
215-676-9494

South Carolina
243 King Street, Charleston, SC 29401   843-577-0175

Tennessee
4811 Poplar Avenue, Memphis, TN 38117   901-761-2987

Texas
114 Main Plaza, San Antonio, TX 78205   210-224-8101

Virginia
1025 King Street, Alexandria, VA 22314   703-549-3806

Canada
3022 Dufferin Street, Toronto, Ontario, Canada M6B 3T5
416-781-9131
1155 Yonge Street, Toronto, Ontario, Canada M4T 1W2   416-934-3440

¡También somos su fuente para libros, videos y música en español!